Are you ready for an Art Attack?

Have you ever tried printing before? It's easy and fun to do – and there are lots of different ways to do it! It can be a messy business so always make sure you protect your work surface with plenty of old newspapers and your clothes with an apron or an old shirt.

So if you're ready turn the page and let's have some print-tastic Art Attacks!

CONTENTS

: Antony Gardner   Artist: Susie Johns

D0453041

HIGHLY STRUNG

USE STRING, TWINE OR THICK THREAD TO CREATE SOME HIGHLY ORIGINAL PRINTS!

String prints

1) Wrap a long piece of string around a rolling pin, fastening it tightly with sticky tape.

2) Spread acrylic paint or printing ink over a plastic sheet. Then roll the rolling pin over so the string is coated with paint.

3) Roll the rolling pin over a sheet of tissue paper. Do this in more than one direction, so the lines cross and make an interesting pattern. Leave to dry.

GLUE THE TISSUE PAPER TO A PIECE OF CARD, TO MAKE A GREETINGS CARD.

USE THE PRINTED PAPER TO WRAP A GIFT AND MAKE A MATCHING GIFT TAG.

COVER A SCHOOL BOOK.

String blocks

A simple pattern, repeated all over a piece of paper, is called a repeat pattern! It's how a lot of wallpapers and fabrics are printed. Make your own design with cardboard and string and repeat it to make patterned paper that could be used as wrapping paper, a book covering or anything you wish!

You will need:

thick cardboard box card,
acrylic paints or printing inks,
sheet of plastic,
coloured paper,
string,
PVA glue,
roller.

1) Cut the cardboard into squares. These can be any size but 3cm or 4cm is easy to handle.

2) Dip pieces of string in PVA glue and stick on to card squares, creating simple shapes. Leave to dry thoroughly.

3) Roll out some printing ink or paint on a sheet of plastic, then roll the ink on to the printing block you've made, so the string is well coated.

4) Press the block on to paper and lift off, to make a print. Repeat until you have covered the paper. Leave to dry.

Top Tips!

Keep your pattern simple. The simplest designs are often the most effective. Instead of repeating the same pattern all over the paper, why not combine two or more designs?

DIARY

5

POTATO PRINTS

STRANGE AS IT MAY SEEM, A POTATO MAKES AN IDEAL PRINTING BLOCK! MAKE SURE YOU ASK AN ADULT FOR HELP WHEN CUTTING OUT SHAPES IN THE POTATO.

JUST SLICE A POTATO IN HALF THEN CUT OUT SHAPES, DIP INTO PAINT AND PRINT. TRY OUT A FEW DESIGNS ON PAPER FIRST BEFORE DECORATING YOUR ART ATTACK OR IDEA.

You will need:

Potatoes, felt tip, paints, paper, roller.

How to make a potato print...

1) Carefully slice a large potato in half - ask an adult to help you.

2) Draw your design on the cut surface, using a felt tip pen.

3) Cut away any parts of the potato that you don't wish to print. Do very small sections at a time.

4) Wipe the potato to get rid of as much moisture as possible.

5) Dip the potato in paint or roll paint on to the potato. If you roll paint on in small sections, you can use different colours and make a multi-coloured print like the leaves of this tree.

To make this fish print...

1) Cut a basic fish shape in your potato half and print it in your first colour.

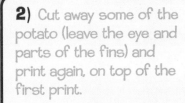

2) Cut away some of the potato (leave the eye and parts of the fins) and print again, on top of the first print.

3) Cut away even more potato and print again, in a third colour.

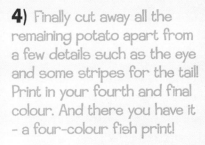

4) Finally cut away all the remaining potato apart from a few details such as the eye and some stripes for the tail! Print in your fourth and final colour. And there you have it - a four-colour fish print!

TRY IT YOURSELF!

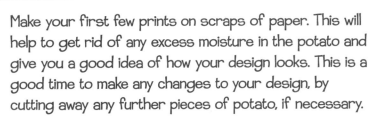

Top Tips!

Make your first few prints on scraps of paper. This will help to get rid of any excess moisture in the potato and give you a good idea of how your design looks. This is a good time to make any changes to your design, by cutting away any further pieces of potato, if necessary.

Do not use too much paint! You only need to cover the potato with a thin layer - too much paint, and it will squidge out when you make a print.

Always ask an adult to help with cutting the potato. It can be quite tricky to cut an intricate design - and you don't want to cut yourself!

TEE-RRIFFIC TOP

A PLAIN WHITE T-SHIRT CAN BE TRANSFORMED WITH SOME UNIQUE PRINTS. YOU CAN USE POTATOES, FOAM, CARDBOARD OR SPONGE TO MAKE YOUR PRINTING BLOCK. COPY THESE IDEAS OR THINK UP A FEW OF YOUR OWN!

GAME ON

MAKE THE FOLLOWING SHAPES FROM POTATOES: head, arm, L-shape for leg, shirt, shorts, small rectangle for sock, boot and a round shape for the ball.

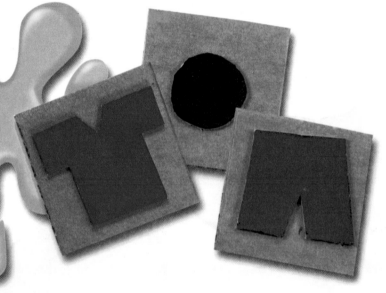

1) Protect your work surface with plenty of newspaper. Place a sheet of cardboard or a thick wad of paper inside the T-shirt so that the fabric paint does not soak through to the back.

2) Start by printing the shirt and shorts. Dip the shirt shape in red fabric paint and press on to the fabric. Print it two or more times. Then dip the shorts shape in blue fabric paint and print underneath each shirt shape.

3) Dip the head shape in skin coloured paint and print. Repeat with the arm. The L-shape can be reversed, enabling it to print both the right and left legs!

4) Print a sock shape in red at the end of each leg, and black boots. Then print a ball and you will have a football game to wear across your chest!

5) Finally, leave the paint to dry and iron the T-shirt, which will fix the paint, so it won't wash out next time your T-shirt goes in the washing machine!

You will need:

2 or 3 large potatoes,
fabric paints in blue, red, skin colour,
black, green, pink, cotton
T-shirt, cardboard,
newspapers.

PETAL POWER

Cut a simple petal shape
which can also be used for
leaves (just wash off one
colour, then print with
another!)

Print a round shape for
flower centres, surround
with petals, then print
stems and leaves. Easy!

FABRIC PAINTS

Fabric paints are available from craft shops. You only
need to buy a few basic colours to start with - red,
yellow, blue and black - as other colours can be mixed.
Follow the manufacturer's instructions carefully. You
usually have to leave your printed fabric to dry
thoroughly, then iron it with a hot iron to 'set' the
colours and make them machine washable.

They work best on cotton fabrics, so make sure your
T-shirt is cotton! Also make sure it has been washed
before you start because the fabric paints do not
work very well on new, unwashed fabric!

HANDY PRINTS

SOME OF THE BEST PRINTS CAN BE MADE JUST USING YOU AS THE PRINTER! ALL YOU NEED ARE YOUR FINGERS, HANDS AND FEET!

MAKE SURE YOU ASK AN ADULT FIRST BEFORE YOU GET STUCK INTO ALL THAT PAINT. COVER WORK SURFACES AND WEAR PROTECTIVE CLOTHING.

FINGER FUN!

1) Set out all the different colours of paint that you want to use. You can either put some on a plate or dip your finger in the pot.

2) You can draw a faint pencil line of the picture on paper or just imagine the shape in your head.

3) Start with a yellow blob at the top of the page for the centre of the flower. Add pink blobs for petals.

4) The stem is made from green blobs and the pot is created out of blue blobs. Now leave it to dry.

5) Add a thin row of orange blobs to decorate the blue pot and add darker pink blobs to give the petals some shadows. Leave it to dry.

6) Finally outline the whole thing with black pen adding some detail to the leaves.

10

Hands and feet, paints and paper.

NOW YOU'VE GOT THE HANG OF IT, TRY PAINTING THIS COLOURFUL PARROT JUST USING YOUR FINGERS.

1) Draw the outline lightly with pencil.

2) Begin to fill the parrot in with red, orange and blue dots. Create a brown tree branch.

3) Leave to dry and then add some feet, a beak and some eyes.

4) Finally add a border.

HANDS & FEET!

MAKE HANDS AND FEET PRINTS BY BRUSHING ON PAINT AND PRESSING DOWN HARD ONTO PAPER.

DO NOT WALK AROUND OR TOUCH ANYTHING WHILE YOU HAVE PAINT ON!

STAMP YOUR MARK

MAKE YOUR OWN STAMPS FROM FOAM AND RUBBER - THEY'RE FUN TO MAKE AND EVEN MORE FUN TO USE! THE IDEA IS THAT YOU CAN MAKE A SINGLE STAMP WHICH CAN BE USED OVER AND OVER AGAIN.

FOAM STAMPS

TRY CUTTING SPONGES INTO SHAPES OR LETTERS...

Cut a washing-up sponge into letter shapes, dip into paint, and print! To keep your hands clean, stick the sponge to a thick card square.

Make name plaques, book covers, wrapping paper, greetings cards, anything!

HOW ABOUT MAKING A HUGE POSTER OR MAKE INVITES USING A PRINTED SPONGE BACKGROUND...

1) Simply cover a piece of card with a brick print. Create this by using a rectangular sponge dipped into brick coloured paint. Cover the card and leave it to dry.

2) Cut out different coloured letters from old magazines and stick them onto plain paper to create your message.

3) Rip the paper round the edges and then pin or stick this to the brick printed card background.

ANOTHER WAY TO USE SPONGES IS TO WRAP PIECES AROUND A STICK OR SKEWER AND TIE IN PLACE...

Now simply dip into paint and create some sponge pictures.

RUBBER STAMPS

COLLECT SOME OLD RUBBERS, DIFFERENT
SHAPES AND SIZES - THESE MAKE GREAT
INSTANT STAMPS!

The round rubber on the end of a pencil is
perfect for printing small, round spots! And a
square chunk cut from an eraser is great for
printing square blocks!

Combine the two to make a pattern - blue squares
and red dots, for example! Then stick your pattern
on an empty cocoa tin to make a printed pencil pot!

Or cut an eraser into a square
and a rectangle. Print blue
squares alternating with red and
yellow rectangles.

Make wrapping paper,
backgrounds for collages,
picture borders, anything!

Top Tips!

If you stick sponge stamps onto plastic lids
rather than card you can wash them.

Use bits of rough sponge dipped in white paint
to create clouds - the texture is just right.

After dipping the stamps in sponge, make
a couple of prints on spare paper to get
rid of any excess paint.

SUPER STENCILS

USE THICK PAPER, CARD OR PLASTIC SHEETS TO MAKE SOME SUPER STENCILS. THERE ARE A FEW IDEAS BELOW BUT YOU COULD COME UP WITH ALL SORTS OF DIFFERENT DESIGNS!

1) Draw your stencils using a pencil and then carefully cut the shapes out. Get an adult to cut out any difficult bits.

2) Lay the stencil on the surface you want to decorate then hold firmly or secure with masking tape.

3) Dip an old, thick brush into some paint. Remove some of the paint first by dabbing it onto some spare paper or tissue.

4) Now dab the brush over the stencil in a 'stippling' motion (dotting.)

5) Carefully remove the stencil without smudging the paint. If you are unsure that you can do this, leave it to dry first.

HOW ABOUT DECORATING SOME PLAIN PAPER AND ENVELOPES AND TRANSFORM THEM INTO SOME STYLISH STATIONERY?

TACK

You will need:

Thick paper, card or plastic sheets, pencil, scissors, paints.

ART ATTACK Poster Paint

ART ATTACK Poster Pa...

ART ATTACK Poster Paint

ART ATTACK Poster Paint

Neil Buchanan
Art Attack
TV Centre

Top Tips!

Hold your stencil securely otherwise it will slip and your stencil will smudge. To remove, lift one corner and peel away gently.

Keep stencils very simple - if they're too detailed you won't be able to cut them out.

Use an old, thick paintbrush. The best way to apply paint is to dab quickly or 'stipple' through the stencil; this would ruin a good paintbrush and not work well with a fine brush.

BUBBLE-ICIOUS

BUBBLE WRAP HAS A BRILLIANT, TEXTURED SURFACE FOR MAKING PRINTS.

SHAPE UP!

1) Cut out shapes from bubble wrap. Try simple shapes like this star, fish or heart.

2) Roll or brush brightly coloured paint on the bubbly surface.

3) Now place on a piece of paper or card to make a print.

MAKE PICTURES, GREETINGS CARDS, GIFT WRAP OR COLLAGES!

USE A SHEET OF BUBBLE WRAP TO MAKE A PRINTED COLLAGE...

1) Use a roller to coat the bubbly side of a sheet of bubble wrap with acrylic paint.

2) Press the paint-coated bubble wrap on to a sheet of paper. Press it down evenly and firmly, then peel it away to reveal your print.

3) Use the same sheet of bubble wrap to print different colours. Leave all your prints to dry.

4) Now cut pieces from the printed paper, and, using a glue stick, glue them on to a sheet of thick paper.

FUNKY FLOWER!

DON'T STOP THERE - HOW ABOUT COMBINING BUBBLE WRAP PRINTS WITH OTHER TECHNIQUES SUCH AS POTATO PRINTS?

You will need:

bubble wrap,
paints or printing inks,
sheet of paper,
coloured paper,
scissors,
glue.

1) Cut a circle of bubble wrap and print the flower's centre on white paper.

2) Cut a petal shape from a potato and print yellow petals all around the centre.

3) Use a small slice of potato to print a green stem. Use the petal-shaped potato dipped in green paint to print the leaves.

4) When the print is dry, cut the flower out and stick it on a coloured background.

YOU COULD MAKE LOTS OF CUT OUT FLOWER PRINTS LIKE THIS AND STICK THEM ON A WALL TO MAKE A COOL BORDER.

SO TRY IT YOURSELF - A BRILLIANT, BUBBLY ART ATTACK!

MONOPRINTS

MOST OF THE PRINTING METHODS IN THIS BOOK CAN BE USED TO MAKE MULTIPLE IMAGES - THAT IS, ONE DESIGN THAT CAN BE REPEATED OVER AND OVER AGAIN.

MONOPRINTS, HOWEVER, PRODUCE JUST ONE UNIQUE PICTURE AT A TIME. NO TWO MONOPRINTS WILL EVER BE EXACTLY THE SAME!

METHOD 1

1) Cover a piece of thick card with cling film. Stretch the film over the card and stick down the edges on the wrong side, using sticky tape. You will now have a smooth, shiny surface.

2) Squeeze out blobs of paint, in a random design if you want to print an abstract pattern, or in the form of a picture, if you prefer. Use a plastic knife, or a small piece of thick cardboard to spread out the paint.

3) Try scratching marks into the surface of the paint, using a cocktail stick or the wrong end of a paintbrush, or an old comb.

4) Quickly, while the paint is still wet, lay a sheet of paper on top of your design and press down gently.

5) Carefully lift off the paper to reveal your monoprint!

You will need:

Cardboard,
cling film,
acrylic paints,
plastic knife (optional),
cocktail stick or old comb,
paper.

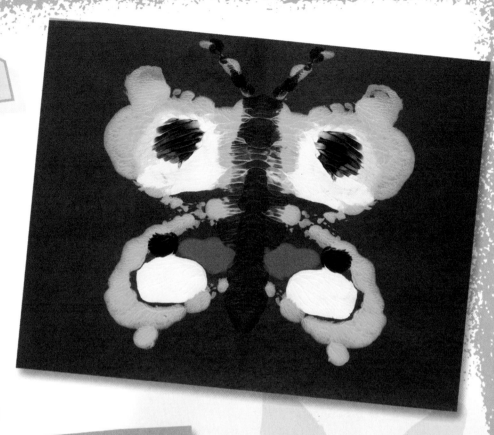

METHOD 2

HERE IS A WAY TO PRODUCE A SYMMETRICAL IMAGE.

TRY MAKING A FLOWER, A BUTTERFLY, MAYBE A SCARY SPIDER - OR JUST HAVE FUN CREATING COLOURFUL SPLATS!

1) Fold a piece of paper in half, then open it out again.

2) Squeeze blobs of paint on to the paper. Use as many colours as you like but be careful not to use too much paint or the result will be very messy!

3) Re-fold the paper, pressing it down gently, then open up to reveal your design.

4) Leave it to dry thoroughly.

Top Tips!

Make sure you lay down plenty of newspaper before you start - this can be a messy one!

Don't use too much paint - you don't have to use loads to make a good print.

When you fold the paper in half, press firmly but make sure you don't rub the paint too much.

FOOD FUN

ALL SORTS OF FRUIT AND VEGETABLES MAKE GREAT PRINTS! MAKE SURE YOU ASK AN ADULT BEFORE USING ANY FOOD AND DON'T EAT IT AFTERWARDS!

PARTY MENUS!

THESE MENUS ARE FUN TO MAKE AND MAKE PARTIES OR FAMILY DINNERS REALLY SPECIAL!

1) Cut a rectangle of coloured card the size and shape you want your menu to be.

2) Cut letter shapes from sponge or foam (use a thin washing-up sponge or craft foam - see page 12) and print the word 'menu' across the top of the card.

3) Cut the pear or mushroom in half, dip in paint and print across the bottom of the card. Add details with a brush.

4) Use the marker pen to write your menu. You could also add stalks and pips to the pear prints.

m...
pr...
roast
pot...
pea...

What a Star!

Look around for fruit and vegetables with great shapes like this star fruit.

Make a recycled stamp pad!

Squash a sponge into an empty, clean margarine tub. Pour some paint or ink on the sponge and get stamping! Make sure it has a lid to cover it up when you have finished.

enu

You will need:

pear or mushroom,
acrylic paints or poster paints,
coloured card,
thin foam,
black marker pen,

cocktail

ken with
s and peas

urprise

menu

mushroom soup

chicken and mushroom pie
mashed potatoes

salad

chocolate mousse

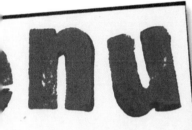

Top Tips!

Don't be wasteful - you can use the same piece
of fruit or vegetable several times - simply ask an
adult to slice off the used layer.

As with potato printing, when the fruit or vegetable has been
cut, wipe it before you dip it in paint as it will be quite wet.

WHAT A RELIEF!

RELIEF PRINTS ARE CREATED FROM SURFACES WHICH HAVE RAISED AND LOW BITS.

I'VE CREATED SOME RELIEF PRINTS BY MAKING INDENTATIONS ON A PIECE OF POLYSTYRENE WITH AN OLD BALLPOINT PEN. THE PICTURE IS FORMED BY THE GAPS THAT THE PAINT DOESN'T COVER. TRY IT YOURSELF!

You will need:

A thin sheet of polystyrene,
ballpoint pen,
acrylic paint or printing ink,
roller,
plastic sheet,
large sheet of paper (bigger
than the polystyrene).

1) Draw your indented design on the sheet of polystyrene, using an old ballpoint pen.

2) Squeeze some paint on to the plastic sheet and roll it out, using the roller. Roll the paint on to the polystyrene.

3) Lay a large sheet of paper on top of the inked surface, press down all over, then peel the paper off to reveal your print!

THE SORT OF THIN POLYSTYRENE YOU NEED TO MAKE A PRINT LIKE THESE IS THE KIND OFTEN FOUND IN PIZZA BOXES!

MAKE SURE IT IS CLEAN (AND PIZZA-FREE) BEFORE YOU START BY WIPING THE SURFACE WITH A DAMP CLOTH.

LEAF PRINTS

Easy to do! Just coat the roller with paint and roll over the veined side of a leaf. Press the leaf on to paper and peel it off to reveal your print.

Cut out the leaf print and stick it to a piece of coloured paper. Punch a hole, add a piece of string and you have a leafy gift tag!

Remember that whatever you draw will be reversed when you print it!

Use a roller rather than a paintbrush because the brush will push paint into all the crevices which is not what you want. The picture is created by the gaps.

MULTIMEDIA PRINT

HERE'S AN IDEA USING THE
VARIOUS PRINTING METHODS
SHOWN IN THIS BOOK
COMBINED IN ONE PICTURE.

WHY NOT TRY IT YOURSELF -
A MARVELLOUS, MAGICAL
MULTIMEDIA ART ATTACK!

The sky is made from blue
paper printed with white
clouds made using a piece of
sponge dipped in white paint.

The pond was made by
creating a string print on blue
tissue paper. After drying, cut
the tissue into a rounded
pond shape and stick on.

The fish is a potato print.
After the print has dried,
simply cut it out and stick on.

The tree, shrub and roof are all made from bubble wrap prints cut into various shapes.

Make a brickwork pattern by using a rectangular shaped eraser. (You could use a small piece of sponge or a chunk of potato.)

The border is printed using the round rubber on the end of a pencil to make the small, round spots and a square chunk cut from an eraser to make square blocks!

Top Tips!

Make the border of this picture separately from thicker card. It will make the whole thing much stronger.

HiNTS AND TiPS!

PRINTING IS A SIMPLE AND FUN WAY TO DECORATE YOUR ART ATTACKS!

MOST OF THE PROJECTS IN THIS BOOK REQUIRE VERY SIMPLE
TOOLS AND MATERIALS THAT YOU PROBABLY HAVE ALREADY
OR CAN BORROW FROM THE KITCHEN! THESE INCLUDE...

paints (poster paints and acrylics)
paintbrushes
sponges
polystyrene packaging
potatoes
paper and card
bubble wrap
erasers
pencils with erasers on the end
string
rolling pin
leaves
cling film

> You can actually buy specialist paints for printing from craft shops.

> These paints are particularly sticky so that they grip the surface well.

YOU MAY, HOWEVER, WANT TO
BUY A FEW EXTRA (AND
INEXPENSIVE) ITEMS, SUCH AS...

rollers (from craft shops)
printing inks
craft foam (neoprene)

USE YOUR IMAGINATION TO FIND
AND MAKE PRINTS FROM ALL
SORTS OF THINGS.

LOOK FOR SHAPED, PATTERNED
AND TEXTURED ITEMS THAT
WILL CREATE PERFECT PRINTS!